T0064558

How about taking care of yourself?

By Paulina Torral

BALBOA.
PRESS
A DIVISION OF HAY HOUSE

Balboa Press books may be ordered through
booksellers or by contacting:

Balboa Press
A Division of Hay House
1663 Liberty Drive
Bloomington, IN 47403
www.balboapress.com
1 (877) 407-4847

Print information available on the last page.

ISBN: 978-1-5043-3270-5 (sc)
ISBN: 978-1-5043-3271-2 (e)

Balboa Press rev. date: 6/11/2015

To my inner self

To my wonderful husband, who everyday helps me and teaches me so much in my spiritual path.

To my beautiful daughters, who have teach me, through their innocence and simplicity, how to live a more joyful and peaceful life.

If you want to know the person that will change your life, take a look in your mirror!

You are what you are looking for.
Rumi

The most important relationship we have,
is the relationship we have with ourselves.

Contents

Introduction

The only intention to write this book is to share, with all the people who read it, how I discovered a new healthier and better way of living as a consequence of various sad and difficult moments I lived. These difficult and sad experiences that I will mention, slowly and silently damaged my emotional health drowning me into a depression from which I came out successfully, thanks to a proper medical treatment and the discovery of spiritual wisdom. I want to share with you how now I am physically, mentally and spiritually healthier by shifting old habits into new habits which I learned from the wisdom of several spiritual traditions, and how they have taught me to take better care of myself. I think learning about these habits can help improve the health and well being of many people suffering from depression or any other emotional or physical disease.

My book is not only addressed to people who is going through depression; it is a book that can help any person dealing with poor emotional and/or physical health, which unfortunately are most of the human beings in this planet, although many of them they don't even know it. It will tell you how to take care of yourself practicing pure and powerful spiritual wisdom. It is a book that can also help anyone struggling with life challenges, and anyone who does not know how to nurture its body, mind and soul on a regular basis. It is basically addressed to all those who lack any kind of self care and thus, have a soul emergency and may or may be not aware of it.

This is not a medical book, it only describes what has helped me for my healing, hoping it can help others in their own healing and spiritual growth. Also it is important to mention that is not a religious book, it is just a book that talks about a spiritual path that can be experienced by anyone, no matter their religious beliefs, as long as they are open to recognize that we are all a Divine creation, full of magical tools within us that are there to help us heal, thrive and live in more harmony. In this path that is available to all of us, you will discover that we all are able to have a more whole and abundant life by changing some wrong day to day habits that we are used to live with, and that have lead us to the exact opposite direction of spiritual growth.

You will find out how and why I ended up with a clinical depression and how I discovered a spiritual path that helped enormously to my recovery, leaving behind the use of antidepressants, and more importantly the practice of wrong habits.

Then, as you keep on reading you will understand why I now say that in my 44 years of life, I have been born twice, one biologically 44 years ago, and the other spiritually 3 years ago, when at age 41 a "new spiritual me" was slowly born.

When you read this book, you will understand that we all have very important spiritual needs that need to be attended in order to really take care of ourselves. You will be able to discover the magic of being in contact with your inner self so you can attend those needs and feel the enormous benefits it brings to us to listen to that inner self and nurture it, so you will never forget about it. You will understand that happiness is not determined by what is happening around you, but rather by what is happening within you. You will learn to be in touch with your wise inner self, which will bring you peace and will teach you, among other things, that you can be stronger, healthier, wiser and happier. As my personal story includes grief, you will also learn the importance of grieving well in order to live well.

You will unlearn wrong habits that all of us were taught since we were kids and will learn to practice healthier ones. You will learn the basic habits I think are necessary to be practiced as often as possible to take appropriate care of yourself.

I am sure that you, as all human beings, have had or has difficult times, but I am sure these habits will help you deal with them in a different and wiser way.

I believe the reason the majority of us are facing soul emergencies, is a consequence of having no schools or teachers that taught us anything about the care of our soul, our feelings or our emotions. We never learned that taking care of them properly is a must to have a healthy and happy life. I hope this book can help as many people as possible to change their wrong habits, as this the only way we will be able to heal ourselves and our society. We all need love and kindness, and in order to be able to give it, we need to first feel it by feeding our souls daily, otherwise we cant give what we don't have.

At the end of the book and through it, I will be sharing information of my favorite books, my favorite spiritual teachers and all the material that has helped me in this journey, which hopefully can also help you.

Chapter 1

"Living Difficult moments without taking care of my mind, body and soul."

Before starting to talk about how I used to live before this rebirth, let me tell you that, in no way I can regret what I did or how I acted in this first stage of my life, nor do I judge myself in any way for it, because I understand now, that I did not know better. Loving myself with my flaws and qualities will now always be my priority and should be everybody's priority.

Now lets begin.

When I was 8 years old, my father started a 11 year long life threatening sickness. It started with cardiovascular problems that caused him several heart attacks during the following years. Luckily he survived all of them, but due to the damages caused to his heart, he had to go through an open heart surgery when I was 10 years old. Living the experience of seeing your dad suffer several heart attacks and going through an open heart surgery at this young age was the beginning of lots of fearful moments I faced all associated with the possibility of his death at any time. Thanks God the heart surgery was a success, and he recovered very well. When he came out of the hospital, he committed to take a lot of care of his heart's health by eating healthy food and exercising every day. Several years after his heart surgery, a kidney dysfunction was detected in the only kidney he had functioning, as when he was born only one kidney was duly developed. For this reason, he needed to go through hemodialysis 3 times a week. Hemodialysis is a very difficult and sad process for the patients who need to go through it as they have to be connected for several hours to a special machine that cleanse their blood and detox it, because the kidneys cant do this function any anymore. Doing this cleansing process during 3 times a week debilitates patients a lot, so it can't be done for long periods of time because the body can not resist it. The only way to survive after certain time of receiving hemodialysis was having a kidney transplant. Hemodialysis did deteriorate my father's whole health and vitality and in just a few months he got weaker and very tired to the point that he could not work any more, and he could no longer do many other mental or physical activities he used to do. He needed a kidney transplant desperately in order to survive. My mother and siblings wanted to be donors, but he never accepted that our health could be compromised because of him, and decided to write down his name on a donors list to receive a kidney from someone that would no longer need it.

More than a year went through with no luck while we kept taking him to hemodialysis. It was really sad for him and us to take him into the hospital for the treatment so frequently, seeing how he was suffering and debilitating more each day, besides from having a very limited diet including liquids. Luckily after one year, we received a midnight call from the hospital to let us know that a kidney compatible with him was available and that he had to be transplanted in the next few hours, so we all ran to the hospital and the surgery started. The kidney was donated by a kind and conscious husband, whose wife unfortunately died during their child's birth. She and him had decided to donate all of her useful organs to other people who could need them when they were not longer useful to her. Here I learned the importance of taking the decision of being donors as it is literally a way to save other's life, and I invite you to do so because their important decision gave my father the gift of living a few more years. As you may understand, even one more single day of life of a loved one is the most valuable gift.

The transplant surgery took more than five hours and I remember we were really nervous of how things would turn out hoping the transplant was a success and that he would not reject the kidney. Thanks God the transplant was a success and my father was the happiest person on earth for being liberated from hemodialysis. He wrote a beautiful letter to thank her donor and his husband, which demonstrated his enormous gratitude for haven given the chance to live again with a healthy kidney. I also was the happiest daughter to see my father starting to recover from the consequences of hemodialysis and to see him with new hope. He and us took great care of him in order for him not to reject the kidney, and everything related to the kidney kept going very well.

A year later, one morning while I was at school he had a stroke that damaged part of his brain. Later that morning, when I came back from school my neighbors told me what happened and that my mother was at the hospital again, so I went straight to meet them. When I entered the intensive care unit I found him full of connections in his head and unfortunately found out that his brain had suffered some damage and that part of the movement of his body was slightly affected. Fortunately he did remember us but had forgotten many things such as math, the days of the week, some speech and many other important intellectual and communication skills. It was really awful to see him like that because he was really desperate not understanding exactly what went wrong with him, and why he did not have the capacity to intellectually understand how he could recover. Neither the doctors, nor us could help him to recover fast, as these types of damages heal very slowly, when they do. It is very hard or sometimes even impossible to explain to someone who suffered brain damage, what happened and that recovery will take time and patience. He needed language therapies for a long period of time to learn again all that was lost in his brain due to the stroke.

As soon as he got out of the hospital, we started with speech and physical therapies. I frequently took him to his therapies as he could not longer drive, and again it was really painful and still is, to remember a father unable to talk to you, to think with you or to chat with you the way he did before. Working, as well as many other activities were again out of his possibilities.

Roles changed in a blink, we now became his fulltime caregivers, his strength and his support instead of him doing his father's role to his son, daughters and wife. As you can imagine, it was very difficult and hard for him to loose his financial, physical and intellectual independence, as he used to be very independent, strong and an admirable hardworking father.

After a very difficult year of relearning and patience, he recovered almost completely from the stroke. He was such a strong person that once again he came out successfully of another health challenge. He demonstrated us again with his example how powerful the mind is, and what a strong will he had to keep fighting battles and keep living. He was amazing and the best example I have ever had of strength and willpower.

Unfortunately after this year of recovery, and as consequence of all his health problems, he went back to the hospital due to a respiratory problem that leaded to pneumonia. This time he did not make it out of the hospital and one morning of May 1990, he passed away. He was 48 years old, and I was 19 years old. This made me the saddest person on earth and my worst fear finally came true, he was gone.

As you can see, I lived part of my childhood and all my teenage years full of fears and stress seeing my father constantly fighting between life and death, thinking I could loose him on any day. I lived constantly worried and sad seeing him go in and out of the hospital so many times getting sicker, deteriorating more every year, and with his health and life constantly being threatened.

My mother and siblings also lived this process very painfully and the worst part is that no spiritual guidance or support was ever given to any of us during all these 11 years. I didn't even knew there was such thing as a spiritual world. My mother, obviously turned all her attention to doctors, hospitals and medicines, and the little free time she had, she had to spend it on working in order to pay our schools and universities as my dad was not able to work any more the way he used to do once the kidney problems appeared. Unfortunately, she had no time or clue of how spiritual wisdom would have helped us to better face these situations, but I really admire her anyway because she of course did the best she could and I thank her enormously for that, as she faced the big challenge to raise us up almost by herself with a sick husband. Thanks to her tenacity, she successfully achieved to provide us with the proper education until we were able to work and help her with some expenses.

I myself felt lonely, fearful and vulnerable during all these years, running in and out of the hospital while studying and trying to live my teenage years the best I could. But the truth is I suffered a lot because I had no idea how to deal with any of these experiences, and while I was trying to have a normal life studying and working, I now know I was not using my inner tools the way I should have to be more positive, healthy and present in each moment. Knowing about them and having used them would have helped me to grief wisely and to have taken better care of myself, my father, and my whole family. Spiritual wisdom would have come in very handy for all of us, but as I said before, unfortunately schools do not prepare us for these types of challenges that life brings to all of us at some stage in our life.

There was almost no communication among our family about the way we could have better confronted this very difficult family situation, or how we could have better managed our emotions, fears and worries. Unfortunately, uncles and aunts have never been close, so no help from them was never received either, although it would have been very useful. Friends of mine and of my siblings were around, but at these young age nobody really knew how to talk about it or how to comfort or nurture us spiritually.

So in all those years, and during many years after his death, I never lived the process of grieving the way I should have. I knew no other way to live but to be frequently sad and fearful of what life had offered me, and of what would life offer me in the future. I tend to live very anxious about health issues and very fearful of death remembering his suffering and mine, instead of trying to remember the happy moments and trying to be more positive. I didn't have a clue on how to take care of myself while all these experiences were happening, nor when they finished and this obviously brought negative consequences to my mind, body and soul in the following years. I now know for sure that when difficult life experiences are not handled correctly, and when we do not take care of ourselves correctly while they are happening, sooner or later they will dramatically affect our souls, our physical and mental health and our whole wellbeing.

This fearful way of living and thinking stayed with me through many years, which drown me more each day, (without me noticing) until it obviously affected my physical and emotional health and made me realize that I was already in a very deep hole called depression, and that I could literally not live like that any more.

It is important to mention that during the next 20 years after my father's death, of course I also lived wonderful moments primarily, marrying my wonderful husband, who by the way has been one of my main and best spiritual teachers and a very important companion during my life, especially in my rebirth path, and also being mom to two precious girls who fill my days with joy and love and teach me wonderful things everyday.

But unfortunately, I lived all these happy years with my past still hurting me silently, with its shadow present over so many precious moments and with unnecessary worries and fears, which if I had learned to handle differently, I am sure I would have enjoyed even more this life stage that followed my father's death. One of the purposes of this book is to help as many people as possible to live without the shadows of their past in their present lives so they don't have to spend years enjoying life partially. Although it is not easy, we need to learn to accept the past, deal with it appropriately and move on.

So what did I miss in order to better cope with all these hard moments and happy moments? Taking better care of myself, knowing better how to handle my emotions, being more resilient learning to listen to my feelings and body needs, recognizing my inner strength, nurturing my soul and taking refuge in it among others. All these would have made me a stronger person, and I think I could have provide greater support for myself, my father and family.

Certainly during all this time I did not took care of my body as I should have, and several physical consequences appeared throughout these years, which I will mention in the next chapter.

Likewise, I did not take care of my mind, as many of my thoughts were managed by fears and worries leaving almost no space for peaceful and positive thoughts. I just didn't know what to do or how to act in order to become a resilient and positive person, and in order to have an adequate mental health to better cope with life challenges in a less harmful way for my being.

And about my spirit, of course I did not took care of my soul either because I had very little knowledge of its existence and that that it needed my care and attention in order to prevent my emotional deterioration.

As you will keep reading this book you will understand why now in my present life I am committed see and live my life in a complete different way, doing my best to change harmful habits for the wiser habits to take care of my body, mind and soul every day. Practicing them constantly is not easy, and I myself have not been able to make them part of my life completely, but the more I practice them the better I feel.

I have learned now that whatever loss you don't work properly psychologically and spiritually, will stay deep in yourself harming day by day your health, and will not improve, no matter how may years go by, until it is properly dealt with. I really hope someone would have guided me before on how to better deal with this very hard stage in my life, teaching me how to obtain the strength and healing that only spiritual practice can offer us. But as the past is gone, and I now try to live more in the present, I can only be grateful that this knowledge finally came into my hands, and that it has helped me to see things in a complete different way. It has allowed me to enjoy more all the things there are to enjoy in life, and has helped me feel more confident and strong with some other difficult or challenging moments that have come up.

Chapter 2

"Living the consequences of not taking
care of my body, mind and soul."

As a consequence of all I lived during part of my childhood and all of my teenage years, when I turned 35 my body, mind and soul were facing an emergency. It came yelling to me as my first panic attack. This was the first sign my body was sending to let me know that it was enough of not taking care of myself, and enough of ignoring the basic needs of my body, mind and spirit.

Other signs that started to appear in the following years included a lot of tension in my back muscles, head aches, digestive problems such as gastritis and colitis and of course my depression. All these diseases came as a consequence of living a stressful life and not handling it correctly or at least a little bit better.

My first panic attack scared me to death, because I did not what was going on in my body and I did not how to stop it or what to do about it. From then on I started to have them more often just coming out of the blue sporadically for no apparent reason. Consequently my husband and I, thinking it was a physical problem, started seeing different specialists to help me understand what was happening and how to stop them or cure them. Different medical opinions were given to us, but no one really got the right diagnosis. All doctors including cardiologists, gastroenterologists, infectologists and general doctors, among others, find nothing physically wrong with me and none of them thought of checking my emotional and mental health, so neither did I.

I continued my life facing them as better as I could with some natural remedies that sometimes helped but sometimes didn't. A couple of years later, besides the panic attacks, I started to feel strange, sometimes not hungry, sometimes dizzy, with irregular headaches, restless nights, anxious, often sad, constipated and with not much energy to do my regular activities at different times of the day or night. Again, I did not know what was going on with me, which obviously made more and more anxious for the health precedent in my family.

Finally my gynecologist suggested that my main problem was psychological. He told me I urgently needed to meditate and relax and he prescribed medicines to control the panic attacks, which I accepted happily thinking this would be the end of the problem. A couple of months went by, and anxiety attacks were controlled but I still felt sad, in fact more sad each day. This situation took me to stop wanting to see friends, not wanting to do almost anything, barely eating, and did not allow me to be present and completely happy with my husband and girls which was really painful.

A friend of mine, which had been through depression several years before, suggested me that I could be depressed and should seek professional help before I could get worse. At first, I had a hard time believing that I could be depressed, having the lovely family I have, and denied it for at least one month. But weeks went by and I did not feel any better, so I finally decided to go to a Psychiatrist who diagnosed me clinically depressed and prescribed me accordingly.

My psychiatrist explained that most of the times, panic attacks lead to depression, and that they usually come hand in hand because one thing leads to another due to chemical disorders that occur in the brain as consequence of anxieties.

Depression is an illness I knew nothing about, so I started reading and learning about it. I learned that unlike some other diseases, you can't cure depression with a one or two week dosis of pills. In my case, the depression was very developed when diagnosed, so it took at least 3 months of treatment for me to start feeling and seeing a very light improvement. Another 6 months more needed to go on with medications for me to feel a real improvement, but it was not until almost one year later, that I can say I was well again.

I consider my psychiatrist a great professional. With our sessions and the medicines duly prescribed and managed by him I came out of such deep sadness successfully which was a very important part of my healing. And I say "part of my healing" because during this disease I read some materials about depression and it causes, and I knew there was something else I would need to work on to heal completely besides the antidepressants, and that was: "spiritual attention and care to my inner self".

Antidepressants duly prescribed by a professional were very important to pull me out of depression, especially when I noticed I had gone really down into it. But besides the medication, I realized I could get best results when used jointly with mind and soul care.

Looking back, I can say that the only one positive thing I got about my depression is that it leaded me to discover this new spiritual way of living. Life found a way to bring into my hands books and information that introduced me to the marvelous discovery of my inner self and all the magic it can do to a person's life. This helped me to feel better each day during the medical treatment, and once it was over.

When my psychiatrist said to me that my treatment was over and I that I could stop the use of antidepressants, he also said that depression could always come back. Of course I did not like to hear that, but with all the research I did about depression and ways to handle it, I came to understand that once the medicines have done their wonderful part of bringing you up again, it is also basic to heal and take constant care of yourself to really cure all causes of depression and most important to maintain you out of it.

This is the day when I committed with myself to practice all that I had read during my depression, in order to take better care of myself and do my best not to go back to depression. It is important to say that this type of commitment is not easy at all, it requires a lot of personal effort every single day. I knew I had to exchange many old harmful habits for the new ones I learned, as it is really the only way to heal and nurture our bodies, minds and souls. I confirmed that many kind of diseases manifest sooner or later if our soul and mind are not duly taken care of, because now I know that the emotional component influences importantly our health. When we don't face our emotions adequately they will keep hurting us silently.

As you can see, depression was the main consequence of not taking care of myself appropriately during so many years, along with some other physical issues. Unfortunately there are lots of people dealing with this disease or many other emotional disorders or physical issues that are consequence of their lack of self-care. It is for them that I want to share what complemented my healing, so that hopefully it can complement their healing also. If you are committed to start working on the habits mentioned in the following chapter I am sure you will obtain great benefits for your whole well being.

Chapter 3

"Adopting new habits in order to take care of my body, mind and soul."

When I finally realized that I had another option different from the one that kept me feeling sad and worried, I chose to change and grow and discovered the spiritual path that lead me to new life habits. It is with these habits that a change in my life has been possible. When I started practicing them, I slowly gave birth to a new me and gradually changed the way I used to see and lived life. Yet, it is important to say that this change is not magical, it does require your full attention to practice them, as well as to remember their practice as often as possible.

As I started to come up from the dark hole I discovered myself in, into the light that I had lost sight of for so many years, I knew I needed urgent attention and more love from myself to myself. I found out that there is always a way to return to the light we were born with, remembering that the sun is always up there even in cloudy days.

Slowly I began a rebirth by learning and reading a lot about self-help, human development, some Buddhism and a lot of information on spirituality and personal growth. I understood that I needed to recognize the good in what happened and look now for all the good that remains. I slowly started to learn to shift my way of thinking, acting and seeing life, due to all the spiritual wisdom that kept arriving to my hands from some wonderful authors.

I have no doubt that when you are ready to change, the right information keeps coming to your hands from everywhere and from the least expected places. I started reading, listening, learning and noticing all about the inner resources our Creator gave us, which I never knew I had within me, and which I had never used before in order to live a more balanced, simpler and more abundant life.

Spiritual tradition wisdom teaches us to reencounter with our souls and our divine inner self, and only then we will be able to discover our divine powers and real inner peace.

One of the first books I read was "Awakening the Buddha within, 8 steps to Enlightment" by Lama Surya Das. This book shares beautifully the wisdom of Buddhism to the western world and helped me start my rebirth process. This book lead me to another one that significantly helped continue my rebirth process life called "Full Catastrophe Living: Using the wisdom of your body and mind to face stress, pain and illness." from one of my now favorite authors, Jon Kabat-Zinn.

These authors as well as many others that I will be mentioning throughout the book have been, and still are my main guides and my main support to keep learning and practicing everyday their teachings in order to take care of myself. Through them and through many other great people, I have discovered the way to live a better life and the habits I need to practice daily in order to achieve this important change to maintain my well-being. I must admit that sometimes I still forget to practice them, but I try to make a daily effort and commitment to do so as often as possible.

When you start practicing them, you will see and feel all benefits that they can bring you and maybe, like me, you wont want to let them go. As I have said, they have been of vital importance to heal and maintain my physical and emotional wellbeing and are the only ones that keep me on the correct life path, which unfortunately many people do not follow. These habits help me maintain in the light, and are the ones who keep me in great spiritual and physical shape since my rebirth, especially when those old habits want to come back, as they often like to do.

In the world that we are living and the terrible things happening all over it, I am sure all humans need to take more care of their body, mind and soul. As incredible as it may sound, healing our emotions and deciding to follow a new path is the starting point to become a better person and the only way to help each other to live in a more loving and peaceful society.

There is nothing more true that when you take care of your mind you take care of the world. The only way to change our society is to change ourselves.

HABIT 1

Changing the way I used to think,
and accepting life as it is

As you have read, during many years I spent my life thinking in a way in which I did not pay attention to my spirit, and in which an important part of my thoughts were negative ones, without knowing that this was deeply disturbing my inner peace and my physical health.

Thinking about the past was a frequent habit in me, as well as sometimes thinking and worrying about the future, and about what negative event could each day bring to me or my loved ones. I sometimes used to view my future and the one of my loved ones in a very fearful and threatening way, expecting the worst and never touching base with our Creator nor my divine self, to instead be confident and positive.

Events such as diseases that could arise to me or my family, or death of loved ones were the ones who most worried me constantly. For many years I erroneously believed that any event that could happen to me, or my family could be controlled by me. I used to think that with my worries or acts I could control what would happen or what would not happen. Imagine all the weight I was carrying on my shoulders! My rebirth process showed me that if I wanted to live happier and lighter I should stop carrying all this worries in my mind.

It was until the beginning of my spiritual awakening, when I understood that if I wanted to improve my physical and emotional health and really be a happy and peaceful person I needed to change the way I was thinking. One of my main guides in this was Dr. Wayne Dyer with all his valuable teachings and one of his many books named "Change your thoughts, change your life".

Changing our thoughts from negative to positive brings enormous benefits, which I personally have experienced. Science has demonstrated that negative thinking can cause feelings as anger, irritability, frustration, depression and anxiety, and can also lower our body's defenses. If you are feeling constantly tired ask yourself if you are having negative thoughts, because one other thing they certainly do is drain our energy.

I recently listened Deepak Chopra in one of his 21 day meditation experiences, saying that our brain physiology is structured to renew itself and create new pathways and behaviors our entire life. He also mentions that neuroscience has reinforced that our brain is capable of healing and renewal. These are great news that confirms us that the thoughts in our mind can always be changed, as long as we send the correct messages and our new intentions. I think it is a much better option to choose to make our mind our friend, which will help us live happily, than our enemy which will block our growth and healing.

Learning to shift my thoughts into positive ones, as often as possible, was possible when I understood that only God is in control of the type of things I worried about, and when I learned that positive thinking is much better for my health. I understood that "what is going to happen is going to happen", whether I worry or not, whether I like it or not and discovered that there are much better ways to spend my life in order to enjoy it fully in the present moment. I finally learned that I do not have, never had and will never have control of many things I thought I did and which made me live constantly stressed. I also learned to change the way I looked at things, so things I looked at could change.

Now I realize that life will keep bringing me good moments and not so good ones, which I can't control, but I need to choose between thinking and worrying about all the bad moments that may come to me with constant fear and stress, or choose to think positively and peacefully about how good my life can turn out trusting that my inner resources are always there to help me cope with life challenges. It is my choice. Although I sometimes forget, I try to delegate this huge task of controlling the uncontrollable to our Creator, (where it always has been), remembering that the Universe is the perfect parent, loving us, assisting us and guiding us even in difficult times. I can tell you there are sometimes I wish the Universe could work differently, so that none of us should go through difficult moments, but as this is just the way it works, I think is better to trust the process of life more positively without so much resistance.

*Trust that the Universe is always
digging in your favor.
Rumi*

I have heard many times that most of the things we worry about never happen, and I think this is really true. Things often seem more difficult in our mind than they actually are, but luckily we can always change the thoughts in our mind. I do believe that our thoughts define how we live because what we say to ourselves whether positive or negative can come to us, and as Deepak Chopra says in one of his meditation challenges, ¨everything you focus on with awareness will expand".

This old way of thinking and this controlling issue was really harmful as it completely wore me out, and weakened me emotionally. And it can do the same to you if you don't try to practice this new habit. It is a very hard habit to practice constantly in our daily routines and requires a lot of our attention to achieve, but it is definitively worth trying as this is the only way to experience inner peace in our minds.

*Your own mind is a sacred enclosure
into which nothing harmful can enter
except by your permission.
Ralph Waldo Emerson*

Another important change I have done to my way of thinking is stop thinking I am emotionally or physically weak, and stop thinking of me as victim for the difficult things I had to live. I have learned that I am not that person anymore, and know that my rebirth has made me a stronger woman which now tries to live and think differently, although sad moments may still hurt. I know now that as long as I am in contact with my true inner self and my Creator, I can have access to all its peace, strength and abundance. With this experience I learned I am stronger than I thought, and so are you!

I think hard life tests will always be better handled if we know that we are strong and capable of handling them with our divine inner resources, because in the end, that is the reason they are sent to us: to demonstrate our strength to ourselves and to grow.

Achieving this new way of thinking requires, faith, optimism and the magic word: "acceptance". Accepting life as it is, every moment just as it is without trying to change anything, nor trying to struggle with the ways things are is a wonderful virtue (and a very healthy one).

When we try to accept life as it is with its ups and downs, with its constant changes, detaching the most we can from everything and everyone, our life flows much more smoothly and peacefully and only then we start to enjoy every moment fully. By accepting life as it is, and trying to understand that the Universe works in divine order, you can live with much more faith and peace. Of course this does not mean that when difficult events arise in our life it wont be hard, but practicing acceptance in our daily life even with little things will certainly help us to better deal with difficult moments when they come up, as we will be able to apply the acceptance technique we have been exercising in our daily routines.

Letting go and accepting things as they are is hard for most of us, as we are used to live attached to many things always expecting things to come out our way. But slowly learning to do so and allowing the natural flow of life to be the way it is, will improve your emotional healing and spiritual growth and will allow you to live with more contentment. We have to learn to let life happen, knowing that we are right where we need to be, and that we are whole just the way we are.

In Jon's Kabbat Zin's guided meditations he talks about accepting every moment of our life, every feeling and circumstance exactly as they are without wanting to change anything, and I think this is really the only way to learn to let go and experience peace. Also the author Tara Brach talks about "yes" meditation, which teaches us to say yes to the present moment with awareness. Yes, she says, is an inner practice of acceptance in which we willingly allow our thoughts and feelings to naturally arise and pass away. Practicing this acceptance, instead of resisting to what is, is a powerful tool to view and live life in a whole different way, because as Eckhart Tolle says, "What could be more futile, more insane, than to create inner resistance to something that already is?"

When we finally start to think differently letting life be, we can then focus our attention in becoming a wiser person, working daily in our spiritual growth in order to be stronger more positive and more balanced. It is really a wiser way to live when we accept life, when we let go of the past and when we live with faith in the future.

It is important to mention that accepting life as described above does not mean to give up on things that can and need to be changed in our life for our own good and for others. When talking about acceptance, I am not referring to do nothing about the things that do lie in our hands and need to be changed, because in these ones we do need to do our best to change and improve them. The acceptance I talk about refers to accepting things that are only in our Creator's hands and that cant be changed by ourselves. This type of acceptance requires a lot of wisdom as the very famous serenity prayer from Reinhold Niebuhr mentions.

HABIT 2

Letting go of fears through faith and trust

Fear is a natural instinct built in us in order to protect us from danger, but when it is used in the wrong way it can be a terrible company. Unfortunately many of us do not make use of it correctly, and are used to live with it without knowing how to control it in order to avoid harms to our physical and mental health. Living without fears does not mean we will eliminate them completely from our lives, it means being able to handle them appropriately in a way that they do not stop us from trying new things and enjoying life, trusting that any time we fail or fall for any given circumstance, we have the inner strength to face it and always come up again.

Living in fear is very exhausting and limits us from doing and enjoying many things. It can be compared to living in a bird`s cage, where you are the bird who was born to be free, but your fear is the cage you put yourself into, that does not allow you to go out and enjoy the many positive and safe things life has. When you start to practice this habit, you will find that faith and trusting the process of life are the only keys that open that cage and let you out to discover your inner strength to live free and in peace. We must learn to choose faith instead of fear when the latter wants to come into our mind.

In order to practice this habit and have faith, you do not necessarily need to be following any religion, in fact you may be willing to leave behind some religious beliefs that may be keeping you living in fear and start a spiritual transformation to understand what faith and trust is all about. You can always let go of old beliefs that don't make any more sense to you, as long as you never loose faith in the power of the Source of it all, and as long as you don't loose contact with your inner-self which has a divine power. I definitely think fear derives from not having enough contact with our inner self.

During my fathers illness my faith and trust were in mute for a very long time. I sometimes thought I was not strong enough to handle what life offered me, and thought I was very alone in this situation. When I thought of our Creator, I felt he had left me alone and believed that sometimes He did not listen to me in my saddest moments. But now, learning a little bit more about how the Universe works in reliable forms and the wonders faith do to us, especially in hard moments, I feel and know that none of us is never alone and that we are stronger then we think we are, as long as we have the time to recognize and nurture our inner self. I loved to learn and feel that there are powerful inner resources within us since our birth, which are there to help us face the good and the bad moments. When you know and feel this, difficult times won't change, but instead you will learn that trust can help you face them with more strength in a way you wont harm yourself so much, which will certainly be better for your health. Every hard experience can make us stronger.

Faith will not always answer our questions or solve our problems, but faith will help us trust that whenever we are facing a difficult moment, our soul, which is our connection with the Divine, will never let us fall. We need to remember that we were all born with a huge inner strength that that comes directly form our Creator and that is always available to us. Being in contact with our inner self allows us to let go of many fears and to try to better understand the reason of why and how things happen the way they do. We should never walk away from inner resources, even less, when we are facing life challenges, because it is then, when we need them the most and it is the reason they live within us: to help us get through them.

Knowing that difficult circumstances appear in everyone life's and that they cant be changed is not particularly nice because we all want suffer less, but as this does not depend on us, at least is nice to know that all of us are able to walk through them with more strength, peace and hope through self care.

I myself would have wished for my father, my family and myself not to have suffered so much, and if I had to live that stage again I would at least choose living it with all the new wisdom I have learned. I know that even knowing all this, it would have still been a very hard challenge to live, but it would have certainly helped me suffer less in all aspects. I think it is better to choose faith and trust as your companion through hard times, than loneliness and fear.

Life storms bring us huge spiritual growth if faced wisely, and this habit can certainly help us know that we can come out them successfully. We must remember that what appears to be the end of something, is always the beginning of something new that with time and wisdom will turn in something good for our life.

I know that having faith and trusting the Divine order of the Universe is not easy, in fact is almost impossible when bad events have happened or are happening in your life. Living hard moments in life can easily shake our faith and leave us in state of constant fear and anger thinking what could come next or how are we going to face these moments, but thinking like this is not going to change anything but our good health.

Many times, we human beings do not have the ability to perceive what is more convenient for us, but we need to remember that life does know. Our Creator knows, and in order for us to get what is more convenient in our life He puts us "tests" that we usually don't like but that for sure will result in the best for our personal growth and spiritual development. My depression is not something that I would have wished for, but it is because of it, that I entered to this wonderful world of spiritual care. This is just the way life is and there is nothing we can do to avoid this tests, thus we must make our best effort and accept every test sent to us, understanding that they will help us develop the values and strengths we need to work on in this life to live happier and wiser. As Oprah Winfrey once said, "things do not happen to you, things happen for you".

You may say all these is easier said than done, and you are absolutely right. I myself still feel fear many times specially when bad news may come but what I try to do, is immediately remember this habit which helps me calm myself and control my fears better than before.

Our Creator always answers our prayers if we learn to listen and wait for them patiently, but we need to know that we don't always get what we want because He is the only one who knows what is really more convenient to us. I once read that God has three types of answers to what we ask for:

1) Yes,
2) Not now, and
3) No, because I have something better planned for you.

If you analyze what answers you have got in your life, I think these are true, and I myself have been given all three types of answers. Sometimes life has showed me that what I wanted did not came to me a for a very good reason that I could not perceive at that moment, and now I can be thankful for being given another option. Of course getting the no answer is the hardest one to get, but in this case we just need to remember that life works in mysterious ways which are and will always be out of our control and that is better to make our best effort to accept them with contentment instead of wrestling with "what is", damaging ourselves.

The Universe is always listening, we just need to be aware of the signs it sends to us, and work jointly to be able to obtain what is best for us and co-create the future we want as long as it is focused in our well being and the well being of others. The only way to have the precious treasure of inner peace, and to have a good night sleep is to have faith and trust in someone greater than us who created us in this wonderful world.

When you find yourself thinking that miracles do not happen or that our Creator does not work for us and with us, just look yourself in the mirror to see all the miracles that are constantly going on in your body just to keep you alive. Noticing this and many other miracles in ourselves and in nature, helps us prove that our Creator is always working for us and on us, and that miracles can happen every second.

Being optimistic, plays an important role in this habit also, as thinking positively about the future helps us live with less stress and fear and attracts good things to happen with the incredible power of our minds. In fact this is what faith is all about: trusting that everything will turn out well no matter what happens.

Sometimes life can be so overwhelming that you may think you don't longer have the strength or courage to go on. This is exactly when this habit comes in handy, as it will help us know that we can always take one more step of faith and that we are fully capable of getting out of the hard times victoriously. Remember that our Creator knows everything that is going on your life in every moment, good or bad, and that especially in the bad moments, He is there for you every step of the way through your inner self.

I agree that what is impossible for our mind is possible for our soul. The way I see it and the way I have experienced it, is that without faith in our Creator and in yourself, you cant be a strong and secure person, you can't be positive and you can't be joyful. Serenity, harmony and tranquility can only come when faith and trust are part of our life. So instead of asking some may questions about life, start working on improving your faith on our Creator or in the Divine intelligence, and start to trust more yourself and your wonderful inner resources. I think this is the only way to live fearless on an everyday basis. Living in constant fear makes no sense because as Arianna Huffington says in one of her guided meditations: "In the coldest of winter days there is no reason to worry that spring wont come; there is reason to keep us warm until the season changes". We need to learn to trust that things will work out eventually, and instead of using our mind to worry, we must use it to create realistic solutions and think of ways to enjoy more fully the present.

As you can see in the last paragraph, this habit is not only about having faith in our Creator to live fearless, it is also about faith and trust in yourself, which is crucial to achieve your goals and your well being. We need to recognize the power that lives within us and trust that we have the right and the possibility to live our life peacefully, no matter what the outside events are. When you have faith in yourself you no longer allow fears to haunt you everyday, you know you are capable of handling difficult situations for sure with sadness or pain, but with peace. You trust and know that you are part of the Divine and that you do not need to be perfect, nor to have a perfect life to achieve what you want and what you need to grow. As you grow confident of yourself your faith becomes stronger and unbreakable and security and peace becomes part of your daily life and of your future. This way of thinking about yourself is certainly better than the self negative conversations most people use to have with themselves, it allows us to find the light of faith, and remembers us that we are really capable of living and dealing with life ups and downs.

HABIT 3

Letting go of resentments and forgiving

Resentments are one of the main problems to any type of relationship, and one of the main reasons the world is full of hatred, envy and violence. During my rebirth process, I noticed that there were some people I used to judge, some people with whom I lived in resentment with, and some people I had not forgiven. I also noticed that not only I had resentments with people but with life itself, because of the life experiences that had been offered to me, comparing what life experiences had been offered to others. All these feelings, of course made my mind and body sick. When I noticed this deterioration of my mental and physical health I decided I did not want to do this to myself anymore, because I discovered that living with resentments causes enormous damage to our health as well as to our soul. I discovered that living with all the junk from the past was not allowing me to live a whole and joyful life in the present.

Now I have learned that comparing, judging, and living in resentment for what others have and I don't is never a good thing to do. First, because you never really know what others have been through, are going through, or even what they will go through in their life; and second, because it has no use but to make you feel like a victim preventing you to see what other good things you do have in our life even in difficult moments. Also a very important thing that I have learned and try to do more, is to stop assuming things and stop taking things personally.

When I was a teenager and a young adult I sometimes thought of myself as a victim. I also thought that sometimes life was not on my side because of the things and events I had to live, and for how well I thought life treated others. I was really confused by all things that had happened in my life and about how things worked in this world. Letting go of resentments was not in my agenda because I knew very little about how to do this, and the benefits it would bring for my self-care. Shifting to a spiritual path and learning about this habit helped me understand what I have said about the Universe having different plans for each and everyone of us which unfold in Divine order, and which have a reason to happen the way they do, which usually is to help us become better persons and to grow stronger. I know these plans are really painful sometimes and we don't like them to happen to us but living resentful for how life works is not going to change them. In fact, if we pay attention, they generally lead us to our true purpose in life as long as we are open to learn the lesson they come to teach us.

We must understand that each of us come to fight different battles, and comparing or wanting to have others life is not wise, and besides it is impossible. I then started to learn to love my life with its ups and downs and stopped my thought of being a victim. This does not mean I no longer feel sad for the difficult memories of my dad's illness, of course I do and of course I wish it would have been other way, but I now know that feeling resentments with life or feeling as a victim is useless and harmful, preventing us from growing, enjoying and healing. Practicing this habit helps us see that this is a wiser way to see life, as it helps us accept the challenges that life offers to all of us without comparing. It helps us get through the storms of life in a more positive way and when the storms last too long, maybe the reason for that is that no wisdom is being used to better face them, otherwise I think they can be a little bit lighter to handle.

In order to let go of resentments that we may be holding with others, we absolutely need to forgive. Forgiveness is crucial for a real emotional healing, thus is an essential path that we must work on constantly to feel true inner peace. Forgiveness helps us heal physically and emotionally, it enlightens our spirit and lets us out from the dark cave of resentments. I can tell you all this is true because I have experienced all these benefits myself.

In my new lifestyle I try to understand that people acts and words are done and spoken in accordance with their level of spiritual growth and in accordance to their wisdom. So now instead of getting mad or sad for their acts or their words, (that I thought were meant to hurt me), I try to not take things personally and try to accept them as they are, wishing someday they become spiritually wise. This of course is very difficult and its much easier said than done for all human beings because we have feelings that we allow to get easily hurt. I recognize it is not easy to let go of harmful and negative people or their comments. I many times still notice that I am not practicing the forgiveness habit as I should because it is very difficult with certain people, but when I finally do it, I notice it brings so much healing to my mind and soul that is worth to practice because that way no one can hurt you unless you allow them to.

When conflicts arise, (as they often do) I try to separate peacefully from conflictive and negative people, and focus my time and attention to positive things and lessons that I have been learning, which helps me keep growing spiritually. I try to think that these negative people or negative events appear on purpose in my life as teachers, doing just the right things to help me practice my spiritual habits and become wiser.

Remembering we all are humans and that we all can hurt someone during our life, helps me in the process of forgiving. Trying to be more peaceful and forgiving does not mean you allow people to hurt you as they wish, when this happens of course sometimes is necessary to respectfully and with authority speak up and stop them but the secret would be not to allow their acts or words to hurt us. I mention this because unfortunately many people think that because spiritual people are calm and peaceful you can mistreat them, but it is precisely spiritual people who can be the strongest and the one who know much better how to take care of themselves.

When I don't like what people do to me or to others, I now do my best effort to, instead of judging them, taking things personally, or feeling hurt by them, to try to send them light (which is not always easy, but it is certainly better for your spirit) and forgive their acts understanding that they are doing the best they can in accordance with the level of awareness they are living in that moment. It is important to understand that when you decide to forgive it does not mean that you were not hurt or that you now can deeply love those who hurt you, but it means you decide to forgive them in order to liberate **yourself** from the bad moments, so that you can move on with a peaceful life and maybe they can too. And if you think these people can hurt you again, the decision to walk away from them is necessary, as long at it is done with real peace in your heart. Sometimes forgiving can be really difficult specially when we have been deeply hurt, but even then you must remember you are doing it for you own good, not for theirs.

If living without forgiving others eats up all your energy, as well as your creativity and your serenity, why keep doing this to yourself? Why if it damages your physical and mental health? Some of us think that if we don't forgive we are hurting our offender and we like it this way, but in reality the only one we are offending when we do not forgive, is ourselves. When we don't forgive we cant move forward to our well being.

The great book by Desmond Tutu named The Book of Forgiving, invites us to follow a fourfold path for healing ourselves and the world, and affirms the multiple benefits that forgiving can give us. I find this book to be really helpful for all those who don t know or don't wish to forgive. It mentions that research findings clearly show that forgiving transforms people mentally, emotionally, spiritually and even physically. It says that people who are more forgiving report fewer health and mental problems and fewer physical symptoms of stress, and that a person holding on to anger and resentments is at in increases risk for anxiety, depression and insomnia, and are more likely to suffer form high pressure, ulcers, migraines, backaches, heart attack and even cancer.

Forgiving reduces depression, decreases anger, improves spiritual connection and increases emotional self-confidence. So although it can be difficult to forgive, I think we all should give it a try constantly for your own good because when you do so, you are freeing yourself from the prison of resentments you have been living in and doing so you are healing your whole self. When we forgive we are opening the doors to a better future for ourselves.

Please don't think I now live completely free of resentments or that I forgive anybody instantly, because I am still not able to do that. I am as human as you with a lot of bad habits to correct, but the difference with many other humans is that I do a daily effort to include the good habits in my daily life and try to leave behind the bad ones, specially every time I have to face harmful or rude attitudes from others. Doing this has helped my healing enormously, and can help improve your emotional health also. When I forgive I feel more peaceful, and for me that is all that matters.

HABIT 4

Living in the present moment &
learning to practice mindfulness

Living in the present moment is one of the healthiest habits for our mind, but it is also one of the hardest to achieve. Why is it so healthy? Because it develops calmness and mindfulness, bringing us to the very healing peace and stillness that lies beneath the agitation of our minds. Why is it so difficult? Because our mind is used to live everywhere but in the present, it is used to be always planning or remembering things or events almost never allowing us it to be focused just in the present moment.

My main teachers in this subject have been Eckhart Tolle with his book "The power of now" which talks about the powerful benefits of living in the present moment, and again Jon Kabat Zin with one of my favorites books called "The mindful way through Depression".

This last book has been my best guide to understand and practice, as often as I can, the concept of mindful living in order to say goodbye to depression. It taught me that there is a lot of work to do in order to really improve our mental health and enjoy a more joyful and abundant life. Finding out about mindful living helped me rebirth into a completely different world. Mindfulness as defined by Jon Kabbat means paying attention on purpose of the present moment in a non-judgemental way, as if your life depended on it. And as he says, it does!

Being aware mindfully each and every moment we are living, is a very hard work and I would say rather impossible, but you can start trying this habit with little moments of your day at first, and then try to incorporate a little bit more each day to your daily activities. Just doing this in certain moments of the day will bring huge benefits to your mind and soul. I myself am not able to do this for long periods of time, but when I do it for any period of time as short as it may be, I notice benefits to my mind, body and spirit, which of course become greater when I do it more frequently.

The challenge is to just learn to bring your mind to the present moment every time you find it somewhere else. We must shift our thoughts from being in the past or in the future, which is where most of our thoughts tend to be, and try to bring them to notice with awareness just what is happening in the now. One of the best ways to come to the present moment is to notice where your thoughts are and if they are not in the present moment, gently let go of those thoughts, and mindfully turn all your attention into the present. For me, one of the best ways to do this is connecting with the sensations of my body by hearing, feeling, seeing, smelling, and even tasting what is presented to me just as it is in the present moment.

Another very powerful way to connect with the now is to focus on our breath and just notice how the air goes in and the air goes out of your body. This will rapidly take your mind to the present moment, which will contact you with your peaceful and healing inner self.

For me, this was something I had never done and trying to do it for long periods of time resulted quite difficult. Living with awareness means to "unlearn" many of the things we have learned through our life, and start a new way of "being" each day, and stopping at least for some periods of the day our "doing "mode. Living with awareness as much as we can, allows us to do the same amount of things we use to do but more concentrated and with a calmer mind which of course turns out in better results on whatever we are doing, and allows us to come up with better solutions to our problems.

Awareness also helps us improve our patience, which is essential to live with more tranquility and less anxiety. When we are mindfully allowing things and situations to happen just as they are, we no longer want to hurry everything and every one, and we learn to wait with more patience and with a better attitude.

Reading and learning about mindfulness taught me that there is no better time to live at, but in the present, as this will free you from bad or sad memories of the past, and from worries and anxieties about the future. This helps us leave behind the worries, fears and resentments we talked about in Habit 1, 2 and 3 taking better care of ourselves.

I now understand that living in the past and constantly remembering sad moments does not help us heal nor grow, the only way to do this is living in the present as fully as we can. Likewise, worrying about the future is not going to change anything about it, it just prevents us from enjoying the present. Just being in the present moment with myself has guided me to the light that had always been within me, but had been completely ignored for so many years, and it can also guide to you to yours.

Mindfulness helps us notice all the good things life has each and every moment, that we usually ignore, and it helps us appreciate nature's wonders. It helps us to let go peacefully of the past, as well as to accept the future to come at its own pace without worrying, but rather enjoying with gratitude what the present offers to us. It also helps our mind to be more relaxed and stops the usual invasion of thoughts that compromise our inner peace. This will bring enormous benefits for our health as well as for any activity we carry out during the day because a relaxed mind is a much more productive mind.

I see and feel my soul as a powerful inner source that lives within me, ready to give me peace and comfort as soon as I stop my daily rush to feel and listen to it mindfully. The only thing I need to do is focus my attention and thoughts in my inner self, no matter what is going on outside, and allow myself to feel the inner resources that are always available to us to help us grow, evolve and thrive. To better understand this, you can imagine the upper part of an ocean during a storm which is full of movement, but that no matter the magnitude of the storm, when you go deep down you can always find calm and serenity. This is the same with our mind, always filled with thoughts, always in movement, but if we go mindfully in a deep silence and become aware of them, we can always let go of them gently and find a still and serene world within us in any present moment.

I am now well aware of the difference between "being" and "doing" and with my best effort try to be more in the being mode than in the doing, at least at some moments of my day. Living in the being mode does not mean you have to be all the time meditating in silence and away from everyone. It just means that anything you do, you do it mindfully, enjoying it and just focusing on what you are doing in the present moment being aware of all that is related to that activity that you are currently doing which certainly brings more peace to you mind and body. Being mindful requires your attention to be in the present moment, and living in the present moment requires you to be mindful of whatever you are doing or thinking.

Of course there is another more profound way of paying attention to the present moment which does require to stop all you are doing and allow yourself to be in profound silence, which is basically known as meditation, but as this is a very important practice by itself, so I will mention it in the next habit.

Practicing mindfulness will liberate you from the daily rush of wanting to be in your next activity when you have not even finished what you are actually doing, and will let you discover the many wonderful things that you let go unnoticed. Living without mindfulness or awareness was like having a patch in my eyes, that did not allow me to notice how many beautiful things the present was also giving me during difficult moments that I could have enjoyed in order to have a healthier body, mind and soul. Living in the present mindfully is the only way to nourish our Spirit, which is as important as food and sleep to our body and to our mind.

Remember, if you catch yourself feeling sad or angry you are definitely living in the past, because it means you are remembering events or circumstances that happened that make you feel this way in the present. On the other hand, if you are feeling fearful or worried you will know you are certainly living in the future, as you are fabricating false scenarios that in many occasions don't even happen. So when you notice any of these, the best thing to do is to turn your awareness in to the present moment by just focusing in your breath to just be in the present moment.

If you are depressed you are living in the past.
If you are anxious you are living in the future.
If you are at peace you are living in the present.
Lao Tzu

Unfortunately no school includes in its academic programs the subject "How to live in the present moment", because if they did we would really be a different society. I deeply wish some time in the near future schools would consider the importance of all these habits and consider teaching them as mandatory subjects. Notwithstanding the above, fortunately more people in our society are discovering their inner wisdom, and each day there are becoming a bit wiser because each day there are more authors and people, who are learning and practicing mindfulness, changing their life and the life of others in very positive ways. The best way to teach mindfulness while it is not taught at schools, is by setting an example with our own children, so that this can become a familiar practice for them since childhood. Do your best to let your children, friends or family see you act with awareness as frequently as possible and do your best to live mindfully wherever you are and whatever you are doing.

One should become the master of ones mind
rather than let one's mind master him.
Nichiren Daishoni

HABIT 5

Learning to give time to myself
through silence and meditation

I have no doubt that most of the people in this planet need to meditate. Whether we recognize it or not, we all need to reconnect with our inner self and with the Source of creation. We all desperately need to become wiser, and we all urgently need to live more peacefully with ourselves and with each other. I think there is no other way to heal this world; if we want to grow we need to be still.

You should sit in meditation for 20 minutes a day, unless you are too busy, then you should sit for an hour.
Old Zen saying

I have found that meditation is a very healing experience that opens the doors to know myself better, allowing to nurture myself and listen to my most basic needs through silent mindfulness and awareness. There is no other way to check how your soul is doing and what its needs are, but through meditation. When you sit silently and center yourself, you can check what negative emotions may be hurting you, so they can guide you to what you need to do or change in order to let them go and heal them opening the way for positive emotions to take their place. Taking care of our emotions through meditation is essential for our self care. Mediation is a nonstop flight to your sacred inner place, which allows you to quiet your mind in order to contact your soul and truly become a better and more serene human being. In his book Full Catastrophe

Living, Jon Kabat Zinn recognizes meditation as a powerful vehicle for growth, change and healing, and I have prove this to be absolutely true.

The problem that most of us face when we first start to practice meditation is that as soon as we want to be still, we get easily distracted with external things and thoughts that keep telling us to return to our daily doing routines. This is absolutely normal, as this is the nature of the mind, but the secret of this habit is to slowly train our minds to come back from wandering from all kind of thoughts and gently bring your attention to focus on the present sensations in order to recognize our soul concerns and needs.

Unfortunately, we have become a society that does not know how to be still, that is always connected to technology and that thinks that silent and contemplation time is a waste of time. In order to really take care of ourselves, we need to stop thinking that everything else is more important than meditating. We need to remember that positive and calm thoughts, as well as the moods achieved during meditation affect our cells positively, boosting our immune system.

I was one of those people who did not allow time for myself, and could not sit still for more than 3 minutes. I did not know how to be still and how to just let thoughts go by like clouds in the sky in my mind without judging them and without clinging to them. I did not know how to give myself some tranquil time to calm my mind and emotions, until my body and soul cried out for help. This happened because I lost touch with myself, as I did not allow time to feel my inner stillness and to listen to my most basic needs.

So it was until I was facing my depression, or what I call my soul emergency, that I realized I had to do something to take better care of myself and to recover my health and inner peace, through two great persons who introduced me to the peaceful habit of meditation. One was my family doctor who prescribed me meditation, telling me it would take it would take me to another reality which I needed to learn about, and the other was Jon Kabbat Zin, through his very helpful books and meditation CDs which have been with me every day since I found them and which I highly recommend. (You will see that only by hearing to his voice you will start to relax and feel nurtured.)

This practice does not need to be done alone in mountain for hours. It is really a habit that you can do anywhere you wont be distracted by others for short periods of time, that will help you become a better and much healthier person. Once you experience the wonders that meditation can do for your well being, I can assure you that you will find the time to do it at least every other day, and will reserve it as an important appointment with yourself in your agenda. As I have said, disconnecting from the constant flow of thoughts that live in our mind is really difficult, but meditation is a great help to achieve this, and you can do it in different ways such as focusing consciously on nature and its miraculous creations, focusing in the sounds that surround you or in soft music, focusing quietly in your the breath, repeating some mantras, listening to guided meditations or focusing in your physical sensations. The thing is to direct your thoughts gently and mindfully to something different so that they stop wandering and you can experience real peace and serenity.

There are different ways to meditate and different things to focus on. The ones I mention here are the one I have learned, and the ones that help me calm my mind and stabilize my emotions, but I will keep trying different methods as this is a very healing activity.

Giving yourself some quiet time and trying to "hear " the silence, will help you to center and will help you remember that we are one with our Creator. This will take you to a place of serenity in which you will realize that we all are divine beings full of possibilities and abundance. In silence we can find the answer to almost any question. I myself have proved that with a calm mind I can instantly listen to my soul and only by doing this I have been able to live with more peace and health.

True lasting peace and joy can be only obtained by exercising our inner mind through meditation, which makes it stronger and calmer. Meditating with focused awareness helps me open my soul eyes and live each day better with myself and with others. Every time I meditate I obtain a different experience, sometimes more calming and satisfying than others, depending on how concentrated I can get and how crazy my mind wishes to be, but I know the more I practice the better results I will get. Sometimes I don't achieve a full connection because I have many things in my head, but anyway I do stay still for a while which at least helps relax a little for the day to come. I recommend that even if your are really tired or with a full agenda, you try to find at least 10 minutes in your day to nurture yourself with meditation, as this will help you continue with your day more focused and calm and can liberate you from a restless sleep.

Science has proved an immense amount of benefits for our mind, our body and our spirit derived from this wonderful habit of meditating.

Some benefits for our physical body include lowering high blood pressure, reducing body pains, reducing anxiety attacks, healing headaches, and reducing insomnia. It has been said that meditation can provide the rest of up to 2 hours of deep sleep if done adequately. Meditation prevents stress from getting into our body and releases the accumulated stress that is already in it. As you can see, meditation improves practically all of our body's functions, strengthening in a very notorious way our immune system.

As for the benefits for the mind and spirit, meditation increases happiness, harmony, creativity, emotional stability, and peace of mind. It increases our wisdom and gives us perspective. It helps us have more empathy and compassion, it improves our resilience, and it also increases memory and attention.

I think many of us would like to get at least some of these mind and body benefits, so remember if you want to get them, constant meditation is the answer. I personally have witnessed many of these benefits, so I can assure you they do come as a result of practicing meditation. Meditation has been crucial for improving and maintaining my health; it has been a great gift that has helped me with my personal transformation and has showed me the way to take better care of myself. So why not prove this ancient technique that is completely free and can be done almost anywhere?

HABIT 6

Living with Gratitude

Being thankful is something many of us are not used to be, and the reason for this I think, is because we are simply not paying attention to all the blessings and good things we do have every moment of our life, even in difficult moments. I think most of us practice the wrong habit of wanting and focusing on what we don't have instead of focusing on what we do have. Being grateful means to focus on all the good offered to us every day and remember to give thanks for it. I recognize that even thinking of gratitude when facing life's most difficult struggles is really difficult, but it does have a great power to help us go through them.

During all my father's illness I really never thought of being thankful for almost anything. My mind was mostly focused on his situation and I had no idea I could help myself by turning my attention to the good things that were also around me. It never occurred to me, and no one told me, that I could improve my feelings and help some of my emotions heal by finding things to be grateful for.

Now I know that if we focus our mind only on the problems we have, as I did, we leave no room for our mind to be also aware of the positive things occurring in our life, and no gratitude comes in our life, missing all the benefits that being grateful brings to our well being. Living with gratitude has been proved to automatically help us feel happier, as we realize that not all in your life is going wrong. Gratitude helps us put our situations into perspective, learning to see the good as well as the bad. It helps us complain less about the bad things, making our life a more complaint-free zone. In this habit you need to work to decrease your complaints and increase your gratitude, by being aware of all the blessings you have. People who are thankful are instantly happier than those who are not, even though they don't have everything they wish for. It is better to constantly remember our blessings, instead of constantly remember our sorrows.

In the book "Living life as a Thank you", the authors tells us that people who are grateful about a specific thing in their past and who celebrate their triumphs instead of focusing on losses or bitter disappointments, tend to be more satisfied in the present. So for our own well being and for our health, we must try to stop focusing our thoughts on our losses or problems, and instead focus on the good things that may have come out of a past situation so we can find the light that can always be found in the darkness. This is very important to be able to live happier in the present moment, and it makes life better for ourselves and for others.

Living each day with gratitude can help transform our negative thoughts into positive ones, our fears into faith and courage, our jealousy or envy into love, our resentments into forgiveness, our anger into happiness, and our anxiety in to peace. Gratitude is another habit that reduces stress and thus keeps us healthier. It helps transform our reality, by being positive, and thus attracting more positive things. As Louise Hay says in her book "Gratitude: A way of life", gratitude is so very important to one's quality of life.

One easy but powerful way to practice this habit is the famous gratitude journal. Every night or every morning sit down quietly for at least five minutes and think calmly of all the good things currently going on in your life and write them down. Before starting to write it you may think your list will be very small, but as you do it consciously you will be surprised of all the blessings you will be able to write down, which you hadn't noticed before because we all usually take a lot of them for granted.

There are so many things to be thankful for that we ignore constantly, for example the bed you sleep on, the water and light you have instant access to, the silence of the night, the laughter of children, the beauty of nature, the warmth of the sun, the company of your loved ones or friends, the wonders of your sight, the blessing of hearing nice music, having food in your fridge etc. In order to practice gratitude we need to remember these and many other wonderful things around us, and try to be less hard to satisfy. Being grateful allows us to recognize with less resistance that life is worth living with its ups and downs.

I think being thankful with our Creator, is not only fair but necessary. It makes us feel whole because we then appreciate the abundance and generosity of the Universe available to all of us and allows us to feel content. When you are content it is more difficult to get disturbed by life difficulties because you are at peace, learning to flow with life, accepting what you don't have, and being grateful for what you do have.

This is another habit that is not easy, but every time you catch yourself complaining about something, try to turn your attention to your blessings and just thank for them and enjoy them.

Last but not least, I think we should also always take time to be grateful with is ourselves, especially once we start nurturing more ourselves. I think is very important to do so because this way you demonstrate love and appreciation for your person just as you are, for your achievements and also for every effort you make to become a better and wiser person. Practicing this self gratitude and self love feeds or soul and makes us stronger and prouder of who we are and of all we can achieve.

> If the only prayer you said was
> thank you, that would be enough.
> Meister Eckhart

HABIT 7

Resilience

Resilience is defined as the human capacity to face life adversities, to overcome them and be transformed by them. Resilient people know how to overcome the unexpected and then they are able to thrive. This habit is very important, as it help us cope with life adversities in a healthier way. It is built by practicing the habits mentioned in this book, among others.

I am almost sure that if I would have known more about resilience during my teenage years I would not be writing this book now, as I am almost sure I would have known better how to recognize my inner strength, and would probably have not suffered from depression because I would have overcome all those difficult years with more wisdom.

Many of us do not know that we are completely capable to develop these capacities because no one teaches them to us. But is never too late to work on this habit in order to be emotionally stronger and wiser, and that is exactly why I include it in this book.

I compare resilience with branches of most trees, which during a storm are strongly shaken, but that due to their strength and flexibility they do not brake, and when the storms ends and the calm comes back they are still hanging in there, ready to continue with their growth. Like this, resilience in us represents our flexibility and capacity to face the storms of life and bounce back stronger than we were before to keep growing, recognizing and accepting the impermanence of everything in life.

We need to live the pain of life adversities with spiritual strength and trust in our inner resources. Then, we need to overcome them in company of all the spiritual wisdom we can get so we can really transform with strength and peace. All these is not easy at all, just as life is not easy, but as all of us will face difficulties in our life later or earlier, we need to prepare to face them in a way we can avoid harming our body, mind and soul.

This process does not come instantly nor easily after an adversity. Time has to go by so we can patiently and silently analyze the situation, hear our own needs and be alert to the signs the Universe sends us to learn and grow from the situation. In order to best overcome whatever may happen, each situation must be lived very consciously, so we can then determine which path will be the best one to follow in the new life stage that will come, and be able to leave behind certain type of life or situation that will no longer be the way it used to be. We also need to work to get rid of the emotions that block our growth and make an effort to open to the new stage to come.

In order to achieve a personal transformation we need to change our way of thinking, of seeing and of understanding life in order to become stronger and wiser persons. Victor Frankl, one of the main examples of resilience once said: ¨When we are not longer able to change a situation, we are faced with the challenge to change ourselves¨. This is a big challenge but it is possible.

If I would have known this and more about how to be resilient, I would have certainly made my best effort to change the way I was living and the way I was seeing and managing things, instead of wanting to change my Dad's situation, which of course was unchangeable. I now understand that I don't have to live with the past over me, that my past is not who I am, and that I can choose the person I want to become.

So my advice here, is that we all practice some resilience even before difficult life situations strike, so when they do strike, we can cope with them correctly and avoid as much as possible, hurting our physical and emotional health.

Now the question is how to be resilient.

Joan Borysenko, author of the book It's Not the End of the World: Developing Resilience in Times of Change¨, as well as some other authors recognize certain conducts or habits that resilient people share. Some of these characteristics are:

Being realistic. This ability is very important in order to be able to watch the adversity directly as it is. When you do this and accept it, instead of constantly resisting to what is, you are able to analyze which will be the best solutions and ways to better handle the situation and start working on them.

Living with faith. As mentioned earlier, people who have faith in our Creator have the ability to better understand and accept with more peace what is happening, trusting that they are never alone and that there is always spiritual and personal growth in difficult times. Also, people who have faith in themselves know how to feel and trust their inner strength, as well as other inner resources, to help them bounce back into life in a more wise and healthy way.

Being optimistic. Resilient people always see the glass half full. Although facing hard moments, they tend to be positive and tell themselves they we will be able to face and overcome the situation by not loosing sight of all the good there is in life and in themselves.

Having a good sense of humor. Humor helps us see all situations in due perspective. Good humor allows our thoughts to also be joyful and fun, and remembers us that there are still thing to smile for.

Being grateful. As we have said in the gratitude habit, people who are grateful have the ability to focus on the good things that exist in the midst of any difficult situation, which helps enormously to build resilience.

Having friends support. It has been demonstrated that positive friends are of great help and very needed to better overcome adversities. Solitude, on the other hand, as well as negative people will never be good companion when we are sad or when we are facing troubles.

Taking care of themselves. Even in the most difficult moments and even when they don`t don't feel like it, resilient people tend to take care of their body mind and spirit. They try to follow a balanced and healthy diet, they exercise in order to change neural activity, and try to sleep adequately. Also they try to keep their minds busy with positive and fun things to do, they meditate because focusing in our breath calmly helps build resilience in their brain and try to live with more mindfulness. Doing all these helps them significantly to lift up.

Another very important thing we must do to build resilience is to make our personal stories more positive instead of replying our story of grief or suffering. I once heard Joan Borysenko mention that the more we remember the difficult moments, the more we debilitate our resilience triggering our emotional brain in the wrong direction. If we learn to focus on what benefits our stories have brought, like strength, courage or growth and try to find a positive meaning we will then be helping our resilience grow.

So now you know what else to work on besides the habits mentioned in this book in order to be more resilient whenever a difficult situation arises in your life, as little or big it may be. Doing this will help you to better handle and overcome them instead of being anxious or mad, or in worse cases, instead of falling in depression or indifference.

HABIT 8

Helping others

This is a habit that can really help us feel better, because turning our attention from our problems into others problems, in order to help them is one of the greatest remedies for loneliness or sadness. Helping others is one more habit that improves our health and well being, it can add years to your life, it helps lower blood pressure and automatically kindles happiness. It is absolutely true that when you are feeling sad, lonely or down, one of the best things you can do to lift yourself up is helping others, and this way you are lifting others up to.

Research has demonstrated that helping others and volunteering reduces stress and is one of the best ways to get rid of anger or grief. Helping others lets you see your life's problems in perspective, and gives you a great feeling of satisfaction that helps diminish your current problems.

Although sometimes we may think that our mood can't be improved, we should never underestimate the difference we can make in our life and in the life of others when we reach out and help others. We should not allow ourselves to be sad or alone when the world is full of people who need help, love or company.

Volunteering is always useful for both parts, and as Arianna Huffington says in her book named Thrive, "It should not take a natural disaster for us to tap into our Natural Humanity". I think helping others should be an activity we should all plan at least once a month by ourselves or even better with our children, so they can also learn about the gifts of helping others. When I was under medical treatment for my depression I started to volunteer in a retirement home, taking fresh flowers to teach the elderly how to make flower arrangements. This was an activity that they really enjoyed and even some men joined my class. I felt so good when they told me they waited all week for my class, and felt so proud when at the end of each class they joyfully took their own arrangements into their rooms. This activity helped me cheer up and it certainly cheered them up to.

If time is your problem, as it is for most of us, then at least commit to practice random acts of kindness with all those people who you talk to or run into each day. Being kind to others for no reason is a very good way to help others. There are more people in the world than you can imagine that desperately need a smile, and that when you give them any act of kindness, you can definitely change their entire day for a more joyful and hopeful one. So now you know another prescription to feel better and diminish some of your problems: Just help others!

HABIT 9

Exercise, nutrition and sleep

Since we were all kids, we all have heard hundreds of times the numerous benefits that exercise, a healthy diet and a good night sleep bring to our body. The problem is that many people, even though they know that their bodies are the only place they can live in, do not include these life saving habits in their daily routines, damaging and deteriorating their bodies as years go by.

Exercise is always necessary but it is especially necessary when facing any emotional unbalance. When you are depressed or are going through any other emotional problem, exercise seems like one of the last thing you want to do, but as you may have heard, it has been scientifically proven that it can really make a difference in your mental well being. Exercise may even help depression from coming back once you're feeling better, because when we exercise the brain releases feel-good brain chemicals such as endorphins. Any type of exercise is great for our physical and emotional health, and the best one to practice is the one you enjoy the most.

If you are not used to exercise, I would suggest you include it in your daily habits for at least one month so you will be able see how it improves your whole well being including your energy and your mood. Once you experience these changes, you will probably wont cancel this habit from your agenda again, because you will know that no other activity gives you this feeling of well being during your whole day.

Besides practicing any sport that you enjoy, I highly recommend to include yoga in your life at least threes times a week. I for example, practice swimming 3 days a week for my cardiovascular exercise and yoga the other 3 days of week, and rest for one day. When I miss a practice of any of these, I feel completely different the whole day; more stressed, less energized, less joyful and less spiritually aligned.

Swimming has always been one of my favorite sports as I love contact with water and it helps relax my backs muscles instantly. I also love it because it is one of the most complete exercises there are, including as its main benefits stress reduction, tone and muscle strength, cardiovascular fitness, healthy weight, and healthy heart and lungs. It also increases relaxation chemicals, and it is highly conducive to meditation.

Yoga, on the other hand brings enormous benefits to my internal body by healing many organs with every movement and twist. It also benefits my mind in an important way, as it liberates it from worries when I focus mindfully in each movement, in each stretch and in each breath. Yoga improves flexibility and strength in all of our muscles and it fills us with energy after we do it. In fact, specially when you are feeling very tired yoga will make you feel rejuvenated and reenergized.

When you do yoga you are making time to nourish and listen to your body as long as you practice it with awareness. Other benefits obtained when we do yoga are improvement of posture, better bone health, immunity boost, improvement of focus, relaxation of our nervous system, deeper sleep, improvement of self esteem, inner strength, in some cases maintaining ourselves drug free, and of course peace of mind, among others.

There are so many physical, mental and emotional benefits obtained when we do yoga that results almost insane not to include it as a habit in our life.

There are a lot of yoga classes almost every where, but if you cant attend them for any reason, there are also a lot of DVD`s that contain yoga programs that you can do in your own home previous consultation with your doctor. One of the best I have found, are those given by Elena Brower. She is a great and peaceful teacher that has prepared different DVD versions such as Yoga for Beginners, PM yoga, and AM yoga among others. At least 30 minutes of yoga every other day, can give you the rest your mind needs and will relax your tense muscles, especially in those busy days. Every time I do yoga I feel completely renewed physically and mentally and so can you.

So if you really want to feel the glow of health, stop excuses for not exercising and take time to listen to your body and give him what it needs. Remember that if you have time for social networks you have time to exercise!

As to healthy eating I wont say much because we all listen everywhere how important it is for our body to eat healthy food. The consequences of having a unbalanced diet are well known to be bad for our body, for our mood, for our energy, for our beauty and of course for our whole health.

When you learn to love and take care of yourself you pay more attention to what kind of food you are feeding your body. You learn to first think if it is something that will be nutritious and good for you, or if after a few hours of having eaten it you will regret giving your body food that damages it and food that interferes with your body`s adequate functions.

Healthy diets are available everywhere and most of all have read and listened about the basic rules regarding a healthy diet: the more natural the better, the more fresh the better and the most balanced the better. Eating correctly improves your health, you wellbeing and allows you to feel more energized and joyful. If you haven't felt the benefits of having a healthier diet, try one day to choose a balanced and healthy salad instead of food filled with fat, and although it is very possible that you were craving more for the unhealthy food, you will see after a few hours the difference of how you feel with one food or another, and if you don't feel it,at least you can be happy because your body has received what it needs to keep you healthy.

"Let food be thy medicine and medicine be thy food."
Hippocrates

As for sleeping adequately, this is a habit that we must stop doing only on weekends or every other day because science has demonstrated that lack of sleep has short and long term consequences including serious health problems and obstruction of mental well being. Some diseases linked to poor sleeping include diabetes, heart disease, hypertension, mood disorders and even obesity.

I know it is sometimes difficult to sleep well or enough, either because we are too busy, to stressed or too worried, but practicing the 10 habits mentioned in this book during your day will certainly help you have a better night.

A well spent day brings happy sleep.
Leonardo Da Vinci

Getting enough sleep is very important for our immune function, so it is crucial to adjust our itineraries to fit in at least 7 to 8 hours of sleep daily to adequately recharge our bodies, otherwise we are compromising our health and longevity. Some benefits obtained from appropriate sleep include stronger immunity, improvement of memory and clear thinking, boosting creativity, better sex life, reduction of stress, decreasing anxiety, improving our mood and becoming more emotionally stable which is basic for the correct functioning of our mind.

For me there is a huge difference in my mood, my energy and my daily performance when I do sleep my 7 to 8 hours than when I don't. My family know this well, and they know that if I did not get enough sleep I am not going to be very friendly for the day.

So if your goal is to feel better and obtain any of these benefits remember that sleep is a priority not a luxury.

Our body is precious, it is our vehicle
for awakening, treat it with care.
Buddha

HABIT 10

Loving yourself and having fun

All habits in this book should be practiced to improve our life in all aspects, and of course when we practice them we are showing love to ourselves. But the habit per se of loving ourselves is very important and new to many of those who have forgotten to take care, nurture and accept the most important person in their life, which is themselves. Loving ourselves is so not usual for many of us, and maybe when we hear this habit we may even think it sounds selfish to spend time with us and for us only. Others may think they don't need to do it, or prefer to say they don't have time for it, but we all need to learn to love ourselves because otherwise we can't love others. When you love yourself you learn to love you just the way you are, remembering that we do not need the approval from anyone but from ourselves in order to accept us just as we are. Self-love is a crucial habit to maintain our good mental and physical health, as well as to enjoy life. When you love yourself all aspects of your life improve, you feel more joyful and grateful with yourself and with others. When you love yourself you treat yourself better and in much kinder ways, and this make people around you treat you that way also.

Imagine a car that only gets attention of its owner when the gas fuel is empty. Not other part or need of the car is taken care of, no checkup for other levels or the machine within is done because the owner thinks is not so important, as long as the car keeps running. What do you think will happen? Of course eventually the car will broke, because it obviously needs more than gas in order to work appropriately.

Well, many human beings think like some of these car owners with respect to their bodies. They think that just food, sleep and clothes are our most basic needs, (like fuel to a car) and think nothing else is required, to live this life appropriately and keep going. But this is a huge mistake because eventually as the car, we will break down for not paying attention to other needs we have in order to continue living healthfully. These breakouts usually come to us when we are already facing a soul emergency and can have a severe impact in our health, as they had in me. Thus, as the car, we need to attend other aspects of our mind and body by loving and taking care of our soul to keep running. Without self love we cant give ourselves the life we deserve.

During my rebirth process I noticed that during some years I was short of self love, as well as of a lot of fun moments recognizing the damages this had caused to my spirit. A lot of my time was spent on worrying about others and seeing how I could help them, but not seeing; not even imagining how I could also help my soul to be at peace. Living with fears and resentments was a clear reflection that I did not know how to love myself, because otherwise I wouldn't have let these negative feelings harm me so much. I had no idea I could stop and to talk to myself to calm me down and to nurture me. I did not use my right to take time to see the many beautiful things life has to offer us and to have more fun.

Sometimes I even talked to myself harshly judging myself, not forgiving my mistakes, and occasionally not accepting me the way I was. But this is definitely not the path to follow in order to love and take care of yourself, nor in order to heal your soul and mind. We all need to love and accept who we are, always paying attention of course to what we can improve to become better persons and live with true contentment. We need to be compassionate and kind to ourselves so we can be this way with others. When you dont take the time to love and nurture yourself, a very important part of you is being unattended, and for sure some day it will manifest as a disease. You should love yourself like if your life depended on it because it does. It is important to mention that this self-love has nothing to do with your ego or with self indulgence, and it shall not be related to it in any way.

Giving us time for doing what we love and listening to our needs and to our soul is the only way to become a person whole, a person happy and a person full of peace and self-esteem. Starting your self-love journey can be the best decision you ever do for yourself. All you need is give yourself what you deserve since you were born which is love. The way to nurture and love yourself is totally personal, it depends totally on your preferences and needs, but it is definitely essential for you to do it, otherwise you wont be happy nor you will be able to make no one else happy. If you don't do it you will not have nor transmit to others a happy spirit essential to live a happy life. So make time for yourself in your agenda as of today, because you are and will always be your most important appointment.

I for example love massages and try to book one once a month, because I feel so nurtured when I get them and so relaxed for the whole day that it is a great gift I give to myself. Reiki has been also of great help to my well being as it harmonizes, equilibrates and heals my energy, so I also make time for it periodically. I also love reading books so I prepare my room with a candle, some incense, a good light, and a cozy blanket and give myself time for doing it. Flowers are my passion and I love to decorate my house with them so every week I go and pick some fresh flowers for different places at my home, and every time I see them I feel happy that I give myself such small but great pleasure. All these things along with many others make me a happier person and allow me to enjoy more any other activity I want or need to do during my day. Of course the practice of the habits mentioned in this book is another thing I do as much as I can because they play an important role in loving myself.

When you feel whole, content and satisfied with yourself, you just cant hide it, true inner happiness radiates like the morning sun through your shades. When you love yourself you experience a beautiful encounter with a new you that had been waiting for your attention a long time ago. When you discover this inner self you will never again let anybody nor yourself hurt it and you will hopefully never ignore your soul's basic needs again. You will be able to feel safe and secure with only a deep breath that instantly connects us with our greatest teacher, which is our heart.

As for having fun, this is also a very important habit that helps us maintain healthy and well balanced. A simple smile or a good laughter reduce significantly our stress levels, it makes us feel better and improves our mental health. There are plenty of reasons to be fun and positive besides having a good time. Positive and happy people tend to live longer, but most importantly they generally know how to enjoy their life at the most. So change what you need to change now in order to bring more fun into your life, because laughter and humor helps you stay emotionally healthy. They are a powerful medicine for our mind and body as they strengthen our immune system and trigger healthy physical changes in our body.

And please, if you are like me who frequently used to take myself and life too seriously, please start taking yourself and your life less seriously, although never leaving behind the value of responsibility. I have learned that taking life and my self too seriously had no good effects at all in my well-being. It is a hard habit to change but I do try to laugh more at myself when things don't come up exactly the way I wanted them. I try to look at difficulties in due perspective and try to ignore more the little imperfections that may arise. When I achieve this change of habit, I surprise myself of how although things may not have changed or may not come out as I wished, I can still have a good day and can go to bed more serene because I had no resistance or anxiety.

The best teachers of how life has to be lived are children. Get closer to them as much as you can so they can spread all over you their joy to live and so they can teach you how to live lightly. They are very helpful to remember us that most things can be done having fun at the same time.

So love yourself now and forever by making time to do what you love, by respecting and nurturing yourself, and by having more fun. Practice these 10 habits I just shared with you, and commit to continue your personal growth every day you live for your own good and for your loved ones.

Now you know why it is so important to take care of yourself and all the benefits and positive changes it can bring you and how to do it. Please don't wait to practice these habits until life hits you with difficulties or until your health diminishes. I recommend you start practicing one by one, day by day and with time you will see how useful they will become in your daily life. For every daily situation there is a habit you can practice in order to live a more healthier, joyful, wiser and peaceful life. Remember, this is not magic and negative emotions and old habits will keep showing up, as they still do with me, but the secret as soon as you feel anger, fear, sadness, negative thoughts, anxiety or even some physical pain practice the corresponding habit to feel better.

The great teacher and author Thich Nhat Hanh says, we all have inside of us seeds of anger, hate and fear, but we also have inside of us seeds of love, peace, and compassion. It is up to us to decide which seeds we want to water and grow for our own benefit and for the benefit of the world. Ask yourself frequently how are you planting and watering the good seeds in yourself today?

Chapter 4

The difference between taking
care of your body, mind and soul,
and not taking care of them.

In this last chapter, I want you to take a look to the two very different ways there are to live our day to day life based on the habits mentioned in Chapter 3. I just want to show you how with the help of these new habits a normal day can be lived differently and better, and after reading the following comparison you can decide what habits you need to work on to live your life as best as possible. The goal is to adopt them from time to time, gradually increasing its practice in order to achieve calmness and inner balance in our everyday life.

I am sure that there are lots of people living the same way I did during the first stage of my life, damaging their body and spirit with out noticing it. But if you are reading this book is because you are interested in taking more care of yourself and want to improve your well being which you will achieve by changing harmful habits.

I will first describe the type of day I used to live, and which sometimes I still do live when I forget some habits, and then I will describe the type of day I now try to live due to all the benefits I have discovered it can bring to me and my loved ones. I must mention that I still frequently forget many of these new habits during my day because I am so used to the old ones, but I do my best effort daily to increase their practice.

Both of them take the same amount of effort to achieve; with the difference that one has bad consequences for your health and wellbeing and the other only brings good consequences.

It is important to mention that after so many years of living without spiritual awareness it is not easy **at all** to change from one lifestyle to another. It takes a lot of time, discipline and practice. Be aware that during many times of the day, you will catch yourself living without awareness trapped in the old habits, but as you notice this, you can replace them with the new habits and try to practice them at least for some moments during your day. As time goes on, you will be able to remember them more often, and slowly they will bring you more positive effects into your life as they have been bringing to mine.

1. A day without self-care:

Every morning, all over the world, many people wake up and immediately start thinking about all the things they have to do, how full their schedule is, and hurry up from bed without even having time to be grateful for a new day. They get up from their beds in an automatic way, sometimes even grumbling when the alarm clock sounds, and begin their day without noticing so may miracles each days offers us like the fresh morning air, or the beauty of the sky with the sun just rising.

Obviously morning alarms during weekdays are not so nice to listen, but as we have to wake up anyway we can try to do it with less complains and more gratitude. When they take a bath they open the water, take the soap and shampoo, and think in everything else but in the sensations of the body while bathing or dressing. Then, if they have time, they usually have breakfast in a hurry without really tasting the food or being thankful for it, and are ready to take off for school, or work.

As the day unfolds, all they focus on is work and duties, rushing all day to accomplish all of them, generally thinking of future or past problems, rarely focusing on the present. Of course we all need to think of work and carry out our duties, but the point here is that everything is done automatically usually in a hurry and with not awareness whatsoever. They stress and run from one place to another, and as many of us face problems at work, with coworkers, friends and maybe family, which are generally not well handled. In this type of life, these conflicts are generally handled with anger, envy or hate and judging others is part of their daily thinking. Here, kindness or forgiveness are rarely practiced, and people usually complain about one thing or another wishing many things were different.

After school, many parents rush from one class to another, or luckily will try to help their children with their homework, but this is generally done with no calm or mindfulness, missing the opportunity to really be present with their children enjoying their company and their learning process. I think in this type of life we take for granted many things and moments; we do not recognize that every moment is precious and that we should cherish them more because everything can change when you least expect it. Although weekdays are full with obligations, here people usually do not allow at least some little moments for fun or laughter, and sadly not much quality time is given to their loved ones.

By the end of the day, most of them are so tired that there is no way they consider doing exercise, yoga or meditation or to do something they really like to nurture themselves at least for a tiny moment of the day. All they want to do, is got to bed to finish with this day and start another one the next morning to live it exactly the way they lived the one before. When in bed they again are thinking of tomorrow duties, and as you can see their mind had no time to be calm during all day.

Consequently, when it is time to sleep, they will probably get a restless sleep precisely because of these type of life. Many of them wake up at midnight with thoughts of fear, worry or stress which steals their peace and resting time because they don't know how live a more peaceful and wiser life during the day.

This type of day is not healthy for our body, mind or spirit. There was no time for inner self-care or spiritual growth in any way, because not many of the habits that I shared with you were practiced at least at some moments of the day.

There were not much positive thoughts, nor acceptance or contentment of things as they are each day at work or at home. Usually there is no time for calm or stillness in their minds to better resolve the daily problems, no time was given for mindfulness or conscious awareness, and even less for meditating. Generally no forgiveness or non-judging habits arouse, and no trust or faith is practiced for those midnight thoughts that woke them up. No gratitude is used to be shown for anything during these type of days. No time for exercising regularly and adequately is given, and adequate nutrition and sleep are out of their agenda. Generally, this type of life allows no time to help others and does not include acts of kindness towards others.

Thus, as you can see not much self-care was given during the whole day, and one more day goes by without getting important benefits for ourselves. All these happens for the simple reason that we have very well learned all the wrong habits and practiced them for many years, and are not familiar with the new and healthy ones.

2. A day with self-care

This second choice of life requires a huge commitment to begin practicing a new soul centered way of being, and doing it even for some moments of your day will for sure bring important changes for your well being.

The day I will describe is the ideal way of living in order to have harmony and a more balanced life. I say ideal, because it is not easy to achieve and as I have said, a lot of times I catch myself living on the other lifestyle and have to bring myself back in awareness to stop the practice of my unhealthy well learned habits. There is still no way for me to practice all these habits at every moment of my day, but I do try as often as I can.

Here we start even before waking up. Our nights here in this new type of life are, more often than not, peaceful and restful. This may sound incredible to many of you, as you are not used to sleep like this maybe since you were a child, but it is possible more often than you are used to. You really can decrease the worries, fears and stress that keep you waking up at nights just by shifting your thoughts, by letting faith and trust govern your nights and by letting go of the control we want to have in all aspects of our life. You learn to stop fabricating false scenarios focusing more on the peace of the present moment. In this new lifestyle, you wake up less times at night, because meditation and yoga as well as healthy eating among other habits, allow you to rest better at nights.

You can also reduce hours of insomnia when you practice focusing your attention on your breath to calm your mind and to get in contact with your inner divine self. You remember yourself that you are strong and learn to let go gently of thoughts keeping you awake so you can go back to sleep, because night time is no working time! In this new type of life, we now realize that worries at night (or day) "do not" solve anything, but instead they make us more anxious and less prepared and strong for the solutions that may be needed during the next day. We now sleep knowing that after every dark night, there is always a sunrise, with singing birds to welcome us to a beautiful bright day. We trust that we are stronger and more confident than before because the practice of all these habits is certainly helping us to build resilience for any problems we may face. In this lifestyle, at nights you just turn your worries to God, remembering what Mary C. Crowley once said, "Every evening I turn my worries over to God. He's going to be up all night anyway." As we all know, a well slept night is one of the greatest gifts for our physical and emotional health, so when you achieve this you will be able to start a fresh day with more energy, enthusiasm and optimism.

In the morning, you wake up more relaxed than you used to, and first of all try to remember to give thanks for the gift of a brand new day, noticing the precious gift of dawn that the Universe gives us every morning with breathtaking colors. You can also try to take some time to listen to any noises around including cars, birds, voices or silence, and enjoy the sensation of feeling alive. This can only take approximately one minute of your time or more if you want to. If you decide to meditate in the morning, this is the best time to do it when still no interruptions will come in.

After this first morning session, another precious gift that we can learn to be aware of and fully enjoy, if applicable, is to mindfully kiss your loved ones and feel the joy of feeling the cheeks of your children, the lips of your husband, the fur of your pet or the wonders of your own body. Then when it is bath time, you can just try to feel the water touching your body, and the sensations when you soap and when you dress. I understand most of us need to run in the mornings, but doing this wont take more time than it usually takes, its just that in the same amount of time, you will be doing things differently: peacefully and mindfully, which will already start bringing benefits for your health.

As the day goes on, our life duties will be as present as they are in the other lifestyle, but the difference here comes in how we face and deal with them. Here you practice doing what you do normally in a more conscious way. It is important to mention that doing things peacefully does not mean slowly, as most of us think. Peacefully means to do it at your usual pace but now focusing more on the present moment; being aware of everything you are doing, and changing from the doing mode to the being mode.

When starting our day and heading towards our work or school, we may now try to practice the habit of having positive thoughts, pushing away the old habit of being more negative than positive. We remember that in a any contact we may have with other people, our acts of kindness will never be wasted as they will always be beneficial for us and for others, knowing that kindness kills rudeness. Here a better way to face troubles that may arise at work or home, is to listen to our heart before reacting negatively or offensively, remembering not to take things personally and not allowing others comments to hurt us as they used to do in the other lifestyle. This gives us better results to deal more peacefully with them, and we learn to practice acceptance and forgiveness when needed, doing our best to let go of resentments as frequently as we can.

Here there is no question whether we exercise or not, because we know our body needs it and know all the great benefits it brings to us. We book time for it at least 5 days a week because we now really want to take care of ourselves. I always think that if our body works for us 24/7, how can we not give him at least 40 minutes a day during 5 days a week of our time, if besides it will be for own good and healing. In this type of life you make a commitment with yourself to space in your agenda at any time of the day, at least 10 minutes to meditate in order to be in contact with your inner self and hear its needs. Also you try to make time to do more of the things you love and that make you happy.

When you feel you are improving in introducing more of each one of these habits into your life, you can also think about spending some time helping others occasionally. This way you can finally practice a little bit of each habit and be healthier and happier in all aspects.

Of course it is impossible to practice all of them all day, but try to remember them, practice them as often as you can, especially if you are not feeling well in any aspect, and with time they can become your alternate medicine for many physical and emotional discomforts. Slowly they can become part of your personality. The more you practice to be aware in the present moment, the more you will notice what wrong habits you are following, and that way you can consciously change them. Awareness is like a muscle we need to exercise everyday in order to become spiritually fit.

So here you have these two completely different lifestyles.

The more spiritual oriented life will for sure give you the opportunity to rebirth and live your one -time life, with a lot more peace and joy, because without inner peace outer peace is impossible. Be patient and pay attention to what habits you are practicing during the day, and always remember that when you take care of your mind, you take care of the world.

Finally, commit yourself to take more care of yourself by reading the vast variety of books there are for human development and spiritual growth. I am positive that when you are ready, the books you need to read, come "magically" into your hands to teach you valuable lessons that you need learn in that moment. In my case, one book has lead to me to another and this other to another. I consider all of them spiritual tools that have been put in my way by our Creator to reinforce my spiritual growth and to heal my mind, body and soul.

Practice at least for little moments of each day what you have read in this book and others. It is not only important what you know, but what you do with what you know, or in other words not only read what to do, but also do what you read! Every single day there is more spiritual wisdom you can learn.

P.S. Don't forget to share this with everyone you can, including of course children and young people. All of you who are in contact with children and teenagers in your life, please don't ever let them forget all the wisdom and love they were born with; make your best effort to make these habits part of their daily life, and guide them daily through a spiritual path of love, peace and compassion. Make sure to make available to them lots of spiritual teachings, so they don't need to learn all this the hard way once they are adults. Why? Because learning all these as an adult is far more difficult as we then have to unlearn bad habits practiced during all our life. Lets help children and teenagers make this spiritual learning easier and more joyful.

Believe me they are never too young to get spiritual education, and I know this because I am doing my best to direct my girls into this path teaching them with my example these habits as often as possible, and talking about them whenever a situation that needs their practice may arise. They, in return, are demonstrating they can absorb many of the teachings and even better they usually become my best teachers.

There are many times when they do not fill in the spiritual mood, and I respect that, but at least we try to make some time during the week or weekend to read books or listen to TV shows such as Super Soul Sunday which contain spiritual teachings, and occasionally they listen to guided meditations before going to sleep which jointly with yoga help them rest in tranquility. All these habits can only be learned if practiced constantly.

There are many spiritual books addressed to children and teenagers, as well as guided meditations and websites for their age. Try to make available for them this material, which for sure will help in their spiritual growth. Keep searching frequently for adequate books, conferences, educational TV programs and other materials for their age so they can keep walking on this path. This is what I do, and feel proud and happy to see them learn such valuable information, which is essential for their correct growth and development. I feel more tranquil to know they are learning all this wisdom, because these will be the only tools that will prepare them better to face life's good and not so good moments.

I strongly believe in what the Dalai Lama once said about meditation and children. He said that if every child in the world would be taught meditation, the violence of the world would be eliminated within one generation. To this I would dare to add, that also spiritual education in homes and schools is essential to change so many negative emotions and actions from our young and adult society, and therefore increase peace with ourselves and with each other.

Bibliography

Awakening the Buddha within: Tibetan Wisdom for the Western world, by Lama Surya Das

Full Catastrophe Living: Using the Wisdom of Your Body and Mind to Face Stress, Pain, and Illness by Jon Kabat Zin

Guided mindfulness Series by Jon Kabat Zin

Mindfulness for Beginners by Jon Kabat Zin

The Mindful Way Through Depression: Freeing Yourself from Chronic Unhappiness (Book & CD) by Jon Kabat Zin

Mindfulness Meditation for Pain Relief: Guided Practices for Reclaiming Your Body and Your Life by Jon Kabat-Zinn

The Four Agreements by Miguel Ruiz

The Book of Forgiving: The Fourfold Path for Healing Ourselves and Our World by Desmond Tutu and Mpho Tutu

Thrive: The Third Metric to Redefining Success and Creating a Life of Well-Being, Wisdom, and Wonder by Arianna Huffington

Change Your Thoughts - Change Your Life: Living the
 Wisdom of the Tao by Dr. Wayne W. Dyer Dr.

Your Erroneous Zones by Wayne Dyer

The power of now by Eckhart Tolle

Meditations Cds with Thich Nhat Hahn

Everyday Blessings: The Inner Work of Mindful
 Parenting by Myla Kabat-zinn and Jon Kabat-Zinn

Meditation Challenges with Deepak Chopra and
 Oprah Winfrey

Material from Sounds true.com

Material from Soulseeds.com

Material from Hay House Wisdom Community

Meditations for Emotional Healing by Tara Brach

Material for children and teenagers:

Incredible You! 10 Ways to let your greatness shine
 through by Dr. Wayne W. Dyer Dr., Tracy and
 Melanie Siege

Unstoppable Me!: 10 Ways to Soar Through Life by Dr.
 Wayne W. Dyer Dr., Tracy and Stacy Heller Budnick

Planting Seeds: Practicing Mindfulness with Children
 by Thich Nhat Hanh, Chan Chau Nghiem and
 Wietske Vriezen

Mindful Movements: Ten Exercises for Well-Being by
 Thich Nhat Hanh and Wietske Vriezen

Meditations for children Melissa Dormoy

Meditations for teenagers Melissa Dormoy

The adventures of Lulu by Louis Hay

On my way to a happy life, by Deepak Chopra

Tiger-Tiger, Is It True? : Four Questions to Make You Smile Again, by Byron Katie

Fire in the Heart: A Spiritual Guide for Teens by Deepak Chopra

Good Night Yoga: A Pose-by-Pose Bedtime Story by Mariam Gates

Printed in the United States
By Bookmasters